A TRUE BOOK™

Friction

MATT MULLINS

Children's Press®
An Imprint of Scholastic Inc.
New York   Toronto   London   Auckland   Sydney
Mexico City   New Delhi   Hong Kong
Danbury, Connecticut

Content Consultant

Suzanne E. Willis
Professor and Assistant Chair, Department of Physics
Northern Illinois University
DeKalb, Illinois

Library of Congress Cataloging-in-Publication Data

Mullins, Matt.
 Friction/Matt Mullins.
    p. cm.—(A true book)
 Includes bibliographical references and index.
 ISBN-13: 978-0-531-26321-1 (lib. bdg.)   ISBN-13: 978-0-531-26583-3 (pbk.)
 ISBN-10: ISBN-10: 0-531-26321-5 (lib. bdg.)   ISBN-10: 0-531-26583-8 (pbk.)
 1. Friction—Juvenile literature. I. Title. II. Series.
 QC197.M85 2012
 531'.1134—dc22   2011010047

Printed in China 62
SCHOLASTIC, CHILDREN'S PRESS, A TRUE BOOK, and associated logos are trademarks and/or registered trademarks of Scholastic Inc.
1 2 3 4 5 6 7 8 9 10 R 21 20 19 18 17 16 15 14 13 12

Find the Truth!

Everything you are about to read is true *except* for one of the sentences on this page.

Which one is **TRUE**?

T or F   Friction always causes machines to work more smoothly.

T or F   Friction results from attractions between molecules.

Find the answers in this book.

Contents

THE BIG TRUTH!

Climbing: A Friction Sport

Fighter jet

Sneakers use friction to keep you from slipping.

Car tires are designed to grip the road.

This person is about to learn a lesson about friction.

CHAPTER 1

Our World Is Full of Friction

You have probably seen characters in movies or cartoons step on banana peels. What happens next? They slip, of course! A banana peel is slick and has little grip. When a person steps on it, the peel slides forward, taking the foot with it. Why is that? Because there is little friction between the peel and the floor.

More than 75 percent of a ripe banana is made of water.

Get a Grip!

Friction is a **force** that **resists** motion. But without it, motion would be impossible. How can friction **hinder** and help motion at the same time? Friction gives things grip. It *hinders* your shoes from slipping by helping them to grip the floor. This *helps* you move forward without sliding.

Your fingerprints provide friction when you grab things.

Modern shoelaces were invented in 1790.

Friction is affected by the **texture** of things. Look closely at a smooth floor and at your shoe soles. You will see bumps, ridges, and valleys. When you walk, the bumps of the two surfaces run into one another and the ridges sink into the valleys. This causes the floor and the shoes to grip each other, so you step and you don't slip. Without this friction, walking and running would be impossible!

Mountain bikers have to know how to handle friction.

Mountain biking became an Olympic sport in 1996.

Whenever two objects touch each other, there is friction. Some materials have very little friction when they are in contact. Others have plenty of friction. For example, a melting ice cube slides around with little friction on a cookie sheet. On the other hand, a mountain biker on a rugged trail will encounter a lot of friction.

Phone Book Friction

Try this fun friction challenge. Get two phone books. Shuffle the pages together, so that pages from one book fall between pages in the other book. Shuffle as many pages together as you can, but don't worry about doing them all. Now, ask a friend to grab one book while you grab the other, and pull. Can you get the books apart? What's stopping you? Friction!

brake pad

Automobiles use brake pads to help them slow down and stop.

Bicycles and Friction

Machines such as bicycles take advantage of friction in some ways and reduce it in others. Your bicycle has ridges on the pedals to increase friction and grip your shoes. It has rough material on the brakes to grab the wheel rims. Tires use friction to stick to the road.

Other bike parts, though, are built to reduce friction. The pedals are on arms connected to a smooth shaft that rotates with little friction. Chains have polished metal parts to move smoothly.

Wheels rotate on **axles** greased to roll with little friction. People who make bikes use grease and oil a lot. Why? To reduce friction, so that parts move quickly and smoothly. Look around. You can experience and study friction almost everywhere!

Almost every part of a bicycle uses friction to do its job.

Rubber-padded bicycle brakes were invented in 1885.

It is very difficult to push heavy
objects across a rough surface.

CHAPTER 2

Friction in Place, Friction in Motion

Have you ever tried to scoot a heavy table? One of the things you notice quickly is that it takes more force to get it moving than it does to keep It moving. **Static friction**—the friction exerted by a still object—holds the table in place. The table moves when the force of a push or pull is greater than the force of the static friction.

Heavy objects have more static friction than light ones do.

Friction Rules!

Moving objects and still objects follow certain rules of friction. Let's look at the rules at work. Lay a cereal box down on a table and push it just hard enough to make it move. Now stand the box up on edge and push it again. It takes just as much force to slide it on edge as it takes to slide it when it is lying flat.

No matter which side of the box it sits on, you would be pushing the same amount of cereal.

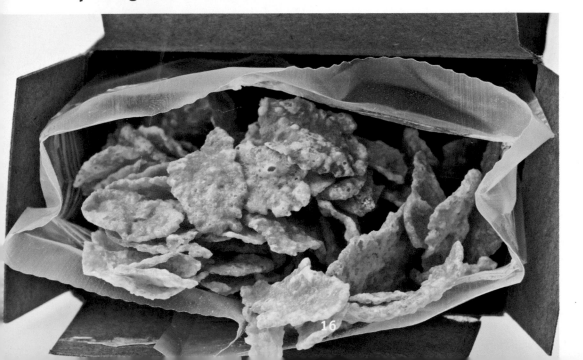

When the box is lying flat, it has many square inches pressing down on the table. But each square inch weighs very little and presses down only a tiny bit. When the box is on its edge, it has fewer square inches pressing on the table. But each square inch bears more weight than when the box is flat. Whether the box is lying flat or on its edge, its static friction will be the same.

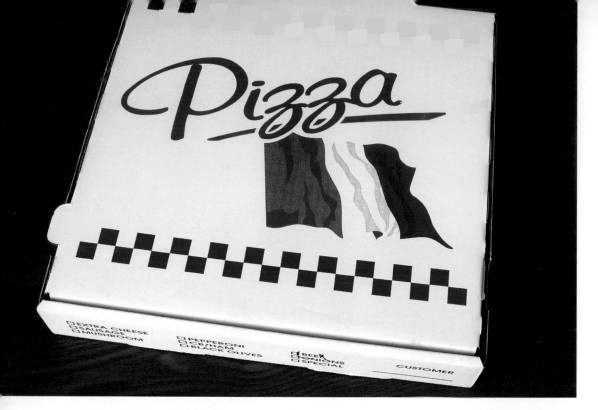

This box requires the same amount of force to move it no matter which side you slide it on.

Friction at Rest

The weight of the cereal box does not change with the box's position. So even though the edge has less surface area touching the table, it still bears all the weight of the box. There is more **pressure** on each square inch of area than when it is flat. So the friction remains the same!

This demonstrates one more rule of friction. The force of friction between an object and the surface it rests on stays the same. This is true even when you change the size of the contact area. It doesn't matter how much surface area an object is resting on. Now let's look at how weight and movement affect friction.

A heavy dictionary has more friction than a lighter cereal box.

Gaining Weight

Lay a heavy book down on the table. Push it just hard enough to move it. Compare that push to the push you needed to move the cereal box. Clearly, it is harder to move the book. It takes more force to overcome the book's static friction. This demonstrates another aspect of friction. The heavier an object is, the greater its frictional force is and the more it resists movement.

It is easier to move the cereal box because it is not as heavy as the book.

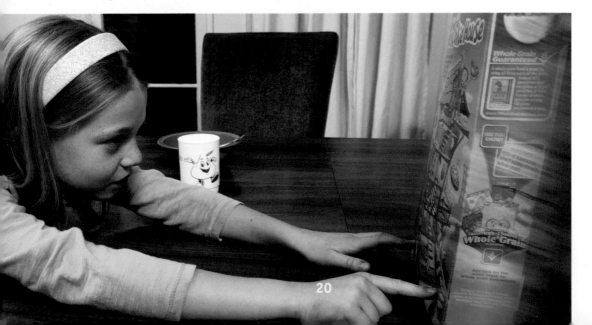

Different kinds of sandpaper are designed to have different amounts of friction.

Sandpaper's rough surface gives it a lot of friction.

Friction on the Move

When an object moves, it experiences **kinetic friction**. It may take a lot of force to start an object moving. But once it moves, it takes less force to keep it going. This shows us that an object's static friction is greater than its kinetic friction. The resistance to motion is stronger when an object is at rest than when it's moving.

Rolling and Sliding

So far, we have learned about static friction, which keeps things in place. We've also learned about kinetic friction, which exists when objects are moving. Now let's look a little deeper.

Some machines use rollers to reduce friction and make jobs easier.

Think about how much force it took to move the heavy book across the table. Now, place some pencils side by side on the table. Lay the book on top of them. Push the book just hard enough to move it. Which was easier—to slide the book or to move it on rollers?

Rollers or wheels can reduce friction. When the book slides, its large surface area contacts the table. Bumps, ridges, and valleys of the book and table scrub against each other. This creates friction. But with rollers, there is little contact between the book and table. Therefore, **rolling friction** resists motion less than **sliding friction** does.

Some kids use rolling backpacks to reduce the friction in their lives.

Rolling friction can be 1,000 times less than sliding friction!

Little Attractions

Scientists tell us that there is more to friction than just surfaces rubbing against each other. Actually, **molecules** are involved. Molecules are the extremely small particles that things are made of. When two surfaces touch, their molecules come in contact. At that instant, the molecules on the two surfaces form tiny bonds with each other.

Everything is made of molecules—even you!

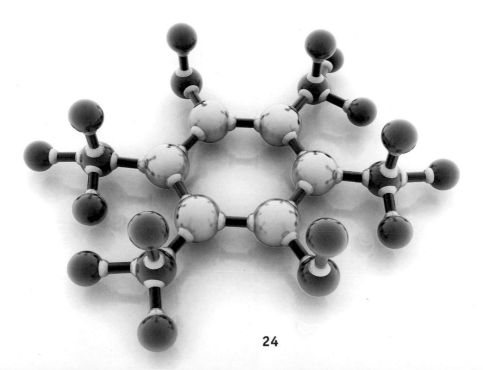

Friction between flint and steel can be used to start a fire.

Knowing how to start a fire without matches is an important survival skill for campers.

If the two surfaces slide past one another, the bonds break and the molecules form new bonds. This happens over and over as long as the sliding continues. If you rub the palms of your hands together quickly, they heat up. This heat comes from the bonds of millions of molecules tearing apart, re-forming, and tearing apart again.

Thanks to friction, these kids can hike up and down hills.

Friction in Sports

Fortunately, we can make friction work for us. Sports would be impossible without friction. If you have ever gone hiking, you have taken advantage of friction. On a steep hill or path, it feels as if you could slide down. But friction holds you in place. The soles of your shoes grip the rocks and soil and keep you from sliding.

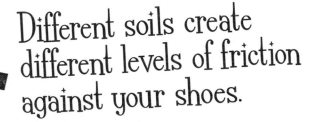

Different soils create different levels of friction against your shoes.

Climbing: A Friction Sport

Have you ever seen a rock climber? Rock climbers are amazing. They go up and down rock cliffs like spiders! They do this by using friction. They grind their soft rubber shoes into the rock to get a good foothold. They rub chalky powder on their hands. This soaks up sweat and keeps their hands dry for good friction. Rock climbing is a friction sport!

Some people go rock climbing in their bare feet!

Climbing gloves often have no fingertips so climbers can get a good grip.

The foam inside a climber's helmet uses friction to stay in place.

Some rocks are slipperier than others. Climbers encounter little friction on slippery rocks.

Cleats help soccer players increase friction between their feet and the playing field.

Let the Games Begin!

Sports rely on friction. In some sports, players wear special shoes that increase friction on grass and playing fields. These are shoes with cleats. Cleats are metal or hard rubber pins that stick out of the soles. Baseball, soccer, and football players use cleats. Basketball players, bowlers, and other indoor athletes do not need them. Instead, they wear soft-soled shoes that cling to a smooth floor.

In other sports, athletes want to reduce friction. Ice-skaters, for example, use thin metal blades under their shoes. The smooth blades offer little friction against the ice. Also, the metal heats up as a skater glides along. This melts the ice a tiny bit and creates a very small amount of water under the skate. The water reduces friction even more.

Reducing friction helps ice-skaters skate faster.

Some of the first ice skates had animal bone blades instead of metal blades.

Carpenters use friction to sand wooden tables, making the wood smoother.

CHAPTER 4

Putting Friction to Work

Work and friction go together. For thousands of years, people made tools to get the right amount of friction to do a certain job. Saws and sanders use friction to do their work. Wheels, however, were invented to reduce friction. Imagine trying to push a big cart without wheels. The friction would make it impossible.

 In 1200, the Chinese glued broken seashells to paper to make sandpaper!

The design of this F-16 fighter plane helps minimize air resistance.

Resistance

So far, we have explored the friction between solid objects. But air and water can also resist motion. When we talk about the friction of air and water, we use the word *resistance*. Air resistance is the friction that works against flying machines. Airplane designers develop machines with sleek lines and smooth surfaces to minimize air resistance.

Boats deal with water resistance. People who design boats shape them to slice through the water. They make boats pointed at the front, and sleek and smooth on the sides, so they can cut through water and move quickly.

A ship's pointed front is called the bow.

Can you see how the shape of this boat helps reduce resistance?

Vehicles and Friction

Cars are also designed to reduce friction. When cars, planes, and boats meet less resistance, they need less fuel. That is because less energy is required to push them through the air or water. Cars that are built low to the ground and submarines with hot dog shapes are built with this in mind. Many design choices are made to reduce friction.

Timeline of Friction

3000 B.C.E.
Sumerians use wheels on sleds to move things.

400 C.E.
Romans design warships to glide through water with less friction than before.

Another way in which designers reduce friction is by using special materials. Some materials create more friction than others. We make canoes, race cars, cookie sheets, and nonstick skillets with smooth materials. We make skateboard surfaces, footballs, steering wheels, and bath mats with rougher materials.

1699
Guillaume Amontons publishes a paper with the two basic laws of friction.

1827
John Walker invents matches called friction lights.

1873
Johannes van der Waals identifies a force between molecules that causes static friction.

If you look closely at a car tire, you can see the gaps and channels that help them grip wet roads.

Designers also combine materials and shapes with friction in mind. The rubber tires on our cars have little gaps and channels. The gaps and channels help slide water away so the rubber can grip the road in a rainstorm. Knobby mountain bike tires increase friction on loose surfaces. Smooth road bike tires increase friction on paved surfaces.

Friction and Machines

People often design machines in ways that reduce friction. The inside of a car engine has many moving metal parts. When metal moves against metal, the surfaces wear down. So we add thick motor oil to our engines. This helps the metal parts have less friction with each other. It also reduces the damage friction causes, so engines last longer and work more efficiently.

Leonardo da Vinci was a famous scientist and also a famous artist.

CHAPTER 5

Figuring Friction Out

Many scientists have helped us to understand friction. In the late 1400s, Leonardo da Vinci defined the two basic laws of friction. The weight of an object increases friction, and reducing the area of contact has no effect on friction. But da Vinci wrote these in a journal he didn't share! It was 200 years before French scientist Guillaume Amontons rediscovered these laws and published them.

Da Vinci drew planes and submarines 300 years before they were actually made!

More Friction Discoveries

Another important discovery was published by Johannes van der Waals in 1873. Van der Waals discovered the tiny attractions between surface molecules. Because there are so many molecules in objects, the "van der Waals forces" cause static friction. We learned much more about friction in the following years. Van der Waals's discovery was named after him. Maybe your name will be on something related to friction someday! ★

Johannes van der Waals was born in the Netherlands in 1837.

Nonstick cooking pans use material that resists van der Waals forces.

True Statistics

Fastest speed of a passenger jet: 1,555 mph (2,503 kph)

Fastest speed of a military jet: 2,275 mph (3,661 kph)

Fastest speed of a land vehicle: 760 mph (1,224 kph)

Highest mountain climbed: Mount Everest at 29,029 ft. (8,848 m)

Deepest ocean dive by a submarine: 35,797 ft. (10,911 m) by The Trieste into the Challenger Deep in the Mariana Trench near Guam

Fastest ice skating speeds: Speed-skaters may reach 30 mph (48 km)

Did you find the truth?

(F) Friction always causes machines to work more smoothly.

(T) Friction results from attractions between molecules.

Resources

Books

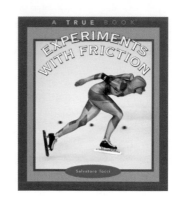

Boothroyd, Jennifer. *Why Do Moving Objects Slow Down? A Look at Friction*. Minneapolis: Lerner Classroom, 2011.

Figorito, Marcus. *Friction and Gravity: Snowboarding Science*. New York: Rosen Classroom, 2009.

Hewitt, Sally. *Friction: Wheels and Brakes*. North Mankato, MN: Stargazer Books, 2008.

Knapp, Brian. *Friction*. Vol. 11 of *Science Matters!* New York: Grolier Educational, 2003.

Niz, Ellen S. *Friction*. Bloomington, MN: Capstone Press, 2006.

Oxlade, Chris. *Fantastic Forces: Friction and Resistance*. Chicago: Heinemann Library, 2006.

Riley, Peter. *Forces*. Mankato, MN: Sea-to-Sea Publications, 2011.

Tocci, Salvatore. *Experiments With Friction*. New York: Children's Press, 2002.

Organizations and Web Sites

Kidipede—Friction
www.historyforkids.org/scienceforkids/physics/machines
/friction.htm
Learn more about friction.

Physics4Kids.com— Mechanics and Motion
www.physics4kids.com/files/motion_intro.html
Learn about motion and forces.

Tribology ABC—History of Science Friction
www.tribology-abc.com/abc/history.htm
Read about scientists who developed concepts about friction
over the last 600 years.

Places to Visit

**American Museum of
Natural History**
Central Park West at 79th Street
New York, NY 10024
(212) 769-5100
www.amnh.org
See exhibits on fragments
of meteorites, which break
up because of atmospheric
friction.

**National Inventors Hall
of Fame**
600 Dulany, Madison Building
Alexandria, VA 22314
(571) 272-0095
www.invent.org/hall_of
_fame/1_5_0_museum.asp
See exhibits on inventors and
their machines.

Important Words

axles (AK-suhlz) — rods in the center of a wheel, around which the wheel turns

force (FORS) — any action that produces, stops, or changes the shape or the movement of an object

hinder (HIN-dur) — hold back

kinetic friction (ki-NET-ik FRIK-shuhn) — the resistance of something in motion

molecules (MAH-luh-kyoolz) — the smallest units that a chemical compound can be divided into that still display all of its chemical properties

pressure (PRESH-ur) — force applied to something

resists (ri-ZISTS) — exerts force against something

rolling friction (ROHL-eng FRIK-shuhn) — the resistance of something rolling

sliding friction (SLYD-eng FRIK-shuhn) — the resistance of something sliding

static friction (STAT-ik FRIK-shuhn) — the resistance of something at rest

texture (TEKS-chur) — surface structure and feel

Index

Page numbers in **bold** indicate illustrations

About the Author

Matt Mullins holds a master's degree in the history of science from the University of Wisconsin–Madison. Formerly a newspaper reporter, he has been a science writer and research consultant for nine years. Matt has written more than two dozen children's books, and has written and directed a few short films. He lives in Madison with his son.

PHOTOGRAPHS © 2012: age fotostock: 5 top, 9 (N. Aubrier), 21 (Corbis), 6 (german-images); Alamy Images: 23 (Rodolfo Arpia), 32 (Greenshoots Communications); Art Resource, NY/SSPL/Science Museum: 36 left; Corbis Images: cover (Al Francekevich), 35 (Louie Psihoyos/Science Faction); Fotolia/Artur Cegielski: 28, 29; Getty Images: 8 (CP Cheah), 37 left (Hulton Archive), 37 center (SSPL); iStockphoto: 11 (Dana Bartekoske), 18 (Brian Doty), 16 (Juanmonino); Matthew Mullins: 48; Media Bakery: 14 (Heide Benser), 22 (PHOTO 24), 10 (Ross Woodhall), 13, 30; NEWSCOM/Russ Bishop Stock Connection USA: 26; PhotoEdit: 20 (Bill Aron), 19 (Amy Etra); Scholastic Library Publishing, Inc.: 44; ShutterStock, Inc.: 25 (Jeff Banke), 5 bottom, 38 (Jaroslav74), 24 (Raj Creationzs); Superstock, Inc.: 39, 43 (Stock Connection), 12 (Transtock); The Image Works: 3, 17 (Bob Daemmrich), 36 right, 37 right, 42 (Mary Evans Picture Library), 40 (Lebrecht), back cover (Andy Mills/The Star-Ledger), 31 (RIA Novosti/TopFoto); U.S. Air Force/1st Lt. Christopher Hoskins: 4, 34.